Patricia Marne is a graphologist, founder member and Chairwoman of the Graphology Society. As a leading expert in the field she is much in demand for recruitment and personnel selection, criminal investigation and other legal inquiries. Patricia Marne has published many articles on graphology, plus several books, most notably *Teach Yourself Graphology* (Hodder, 1980).

OPTIMA

How to Analyse Your

handwriting

PATRICIA MARNE

An OPTIMA book

© Patricia Marne, 1991

First published in 1991 by
Macdonald Optima, a division of
Macdonald & Co. (Publishers) Ltd

A member of Maxwell Macmillan Pergamon Publishing Corporation

British Library Cataloguing in Publication Data

Marne, Patricia
    How to analyse your own handwriting.
    1. Graphology
    I. Title
    155.282

    ISBN 0-356-19654-2

Macdonald & Co. (Publishers) Ltd
Orbit House
1 New Fetter Lane
London EC4A 1AR

Typeset in Century Schoolbook by
Leaper & Gard Ltd, Bristol, England

Printed and bound in Great Britain by
The Guernsey Press Co. Ltd., Guernsey, Channel Islands.

CONTENTS

INTRODUCTION

Every time you scribble a few lines of handwriting you are giving away a great deal about yourself and your character. The way you pen your letters provides clues to your personality; even your signature can reveal as much about you as a whole page of handwriting. Everyone has an individual style of writing – this is why, when we look at a letter we've received, we often know who it is from merely by a glance at the writing on the envelope.

Graphology is the technical term for handwriting analysis. Everyone can learn the basic rules of graphology and in this book a step-by-step guide will help you to unravel the secrets of this fascinating science so that you will be able to interpret the handwriting of family, friends and, of course, yourself. You will be able to bring to the surface many subconscious traits that lie beneath the everyday façade that we all put up. Whether you are young or old, male or female, your handwriting is your visiting card, telling the world what makes you tick and explaining why you think and act the way you do. You could be in for some surprises.

Indeed, many psychologists use graphology as an aid to psychoanalysis when they seek hidden meanings behind the behaviour patterns of their clients. Graphology is also used for marriage guidance, career advice, staff recruitment and for solving emotional problems.

Handwriting analysis has nothing to do with the occult, and the future can't be predicted from a piece of script. Neither can graphology reveal the age or sex of the writer – an experienced graphologist obviously has a good idea of both, but it still needs to be confirmed, as it is very important in reaching a conclusion.

Many features are taken into account by the graphologist including the slant of the writing, the slope, pressure and spacing, the capital letters, margins and signature – they all play a part in handwriting analysis. This book aims to explain some of these features and to show how they can be used to reveal details about the writer.

1
THE THREE ZONES

Handwriting can be divided into three zones. The upper zone contains the ascenders of the letters, the middle zone contains the main body of the letters, while the lower zone contains the descenders of the letters. Ideally the three zones of handwriting should be well balanced, showing a well-proportioned script and a person who is capable of leading a balanced life. If there is any discrepancy in one zone it usually acts to the detriment of the other two zones.

THE UPPER ZONE

The upper zone in handwriting reveals whether you are an idealist and have high aspirations and ambitions, or are practical and down to earth in your approach to life.

Maturity can be seen in the proportion of the upper and lower zones to the middle zone – the mature writer shows no exaggeration in either. If you have extremely tall upper loops you may be aiming too high in your striving for perfection, and your idealistic qualities could lack realistic purpose.

Loops in the upper zone show liberal sentiments and quick emotional responses; you are friendly and affectionate, with a desire for expressing your feelings within

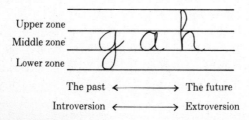

satisfactory relationships. But retouching the upper loops – going over them several times – shows insecurity and symbolises a gap between achievement and aspiration. It is also a neurotic sign in graphology.

If you have extremely small and neglected upper loops, you may be too matter of fact and lack a goal, your logic and your intellect taking over from your emotion. If your upper loops are lean and narrow you could be feeling frustrated, and may even be too rational in your thinking. You may have religious leanings, preventing you from expressing your emotions.

When the loops are thin and restricted, this is an indication of poor imagination and vision, a lack of perception, and stunted warmth. The fuller your loops the more imaginative, affectionate and loving you are likely to be.

Any loop that bends towards the left shows an active inner life, contemplation and occasionally a tendency to brood on memories of past experiences and influences. Loops that bend towards the right indicate intellectual ambitions and a desire to use your mental abilities in constructive ways; you have a lot of push and drive and are career-minded and ambitious.

Very confused and oversized loops are an indication of a muddled mind and, when extremely large, an inflated ego which seeks to find expression by showing off and making a bid for attention. A fantasy mind is revealed – someone who daydreams and substitutes an imaginary world for reality.

Heavy pressure in the upper loops shows a certain amount of mental energy and drive, while poor pressure shows a lack of vitality and, possibly, religious tendencies.

When the upper loops incorporate several different sizes and formations, this can denote dissatisfaction with present achievements, as well as an erratic mind. When a sample of handwriting has a variety of loops in the upper zone – even fluctuating in length – this reveals the writer's tendency to vary his moods. His ideas and ambitions suffer accordingly; he may be optimistic one day, pessimistic the next.

These very tall upper loops show ambition and very high aspirations, but the writer is reaching for idealistic qualities that may be just out of her reach. The small middle zone shows an intelligent personality allowing her perfectionist leanings to outstrip her capabilities; the vision and imagination lack reality.

This writer has little in the way of upper loops, indicating an emotionally responsive nature and a down-to-earth approach to life and love. There is no desire to exaggerate or reach the unobtainable, and the writer is able to function successfully within the environment of home, family and friends.

The loops of this script indicate the use of imagination in ambitions, ideas and relationships, and the ability to allow the emotions free reign (even though the writing has a left slant).

These unlooped letters reveal a realistic and cultural disposition. The writer is intelligent, slightly introspective and doesn't make friends easily, but has the ability for abstract thinking.

These wavy line upper zone letters indicate a weak will and a personality who can be dominated by a stronger personality. They turn to the left, a sign of strong emotional influences from the past which result in the writer failing to look forward or express his own personality with confidence.

THE MIDDLE ZONE

The middle zone of handwriting is the pivot between the upper and lower zone loops. It reveals if the writer is a thinking or a feeling person. If there is a predominance of warmth and affection, or an analytical and logical approach, this will manifest itself in the formation of the middle zone. If can also show the social attitude of the writer with a degree of accuracy.

Someone who has handwriting that is very large in the middle zone is inclined to be self-absorbed, socially outgoing and friendly but egotistical. Such writers are apt to over-react to people and events; generous and extravagant, they enjoy themselves on a slightly larger-than-life scale, sometimes concealing self-consciousness behind a mask of self-confidence. Larger middle-zone writers are aware of other people and like to make their mark in a social gathering, as they love attention and dislike being overlooked.

Smaller middle-zone writers are often happy to be onlookers and are less spontaneous in their friendships – they do not always take people on trust. The small middle-zone writers is a thinking person who uses an analytical approach to the problems of life and love. Such writers keep their emotions in check and don't usually act rashly or impulsively.

Capital letters inserted in the middle zone are a bid for attention; the writer seeks acknowledgment, and has a desire for recognition. Occasionally such capitals appear in the handwriting of creative or artistic people who need to express their personality more than they are doing, the capitals that occur most frequently being R and M.

Because the middle zone symbolises the rational, sentimental social part of the human mind, it measures the everyday reality of life and the social attitude of the writer, giving clues to the way the writer adapts to circumstances, both emotionally and mentally. For example, social self-assurance is always indicated in the middle zone; large handwriting in the middle zone indicates an expansive nature, small handwriting a reserved nature, and medium-sized writing indicates average social relations.

A very rigid or regular middle zone is a sign of an exaggerated compulsiveness; the writer fears to deviate from a stereotype script for fear of making mistakes. This can also be a sign of a schizoid personality in the making, particularly if the writing is over-controlled and angular in formation.

> I think that I should help to build relation the customers, so that they remember call any problems, advising on skin care + help people make the most of themselves happy to say that it is city they are are the links between merchandise + c

This huge exaggerated middle-zone script, without any upper or lower-zone loops, shows an emotionally immature personality whose attitude is liable to be 'me first'. The size and pressure reveal an over-large ego structure and a lot of energy, but the lack of mental agility shown means that the writer acts first and thinks later.

> attainment of a motor cycle, but unfortunately identification, and you have not given your if I am writing to the right person.
>
> meet and discuss things with you, but

This very minute writing is a sign of an inferiority complex. The writer is clever, analytical, reserved and unable to express her feelings easily. There is a lack of spontaneity in the upright script, and the light pressure shows a highly sensitive individual. The wide spaces confirm the emotional isolation and aloofness; any sociability is tinged with caution and a great deal of thought before friendship is accepted.

Thank you for your letter it was very nice to hear from you.

This is an average middle-zone script that is found in the majority of handwriting. It shows a good balance between mind and emotion, and a stable social attitude that is neither too demanding nor too timid. The writer is very self-assured and the right slant demonstrates a forward-looking and outgoing personality.

wrights — something like a It was an excellent product was not as unbearably hot led to believe. On Saturda

When the middle zone is varied in size and the formation is erratic without any consistency in the size of the letters, this is a sign of a changeable and inconsistent nature. This type of writer has difficulty in concentrating and is not likely to follow any kind of discipline, mentally or emotionally.

A narrow or squeezed middle zone indicates a certain amount of repression and sometimes stunted emotional growth. The writer finds it hard to let go and become less constrained. Meanness in money matters is often associated with this sort of script, along with difficulty in releasing tension.

A very broad middle zone with wide letters reveals generosity and a love of space. The writer may be a trifle lazy at times, finding more contentment in taking things easy than rushing around or indulging in energetic exercise.

A middle-zone writing that dissolves into threadlike strokes reveals the manipulator, one who is able to persuade and cajole in order to achieve his or her aims. Such writers are hard to pin down and their elusiveness makes them very difficult to understand as they can be all things to all people. Clever, and usually possessing a talent for understanding other people's motivations, they are highly intelligent and quick to grasp opportunities.

LOWER ZONE

The lower zone in handwriting is the analytical sphere, where the sexual and materialistic aspects of the writer's personality can be detected. The instincts, subconscious impulses and intuitive urges are hidden here, the letters of significance being g, j and y.

These narrow and inhibited loops indicate a harsh, sarcastic and emotionally stunted writer who finds it hard to express emotion. The narrow script emphasises the inhibition he feels.

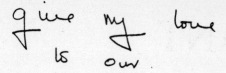

These triangular loops show emotional disturbance and sexual frustration. The writer is inclined to be a domestic tyrant and liable to explode into anger at little provocation. The lack of loops indicates anger, the heavy pressure, mild depression.

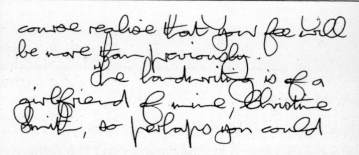

These long-looped and muddled formations on the g and y indicate a lot of affection and warmth, but the writer is unable to control his emotions and they are liable to run riot.

These long underlengths going right down are a sign of some psychological probing on the part of the writer, but there isn't a lot of emotion as the writer is more interested in material possessions and is money minded.

2
SLANT

When analysing handwriting it is also necessary to know whether the writing is left-slanted or right-slanted, as this is an indication of an introvert (left) or an extrovert (right). There are three basic slants – right slant, left slant and upright – although occasionally you may come across a mixture.

RIGHT SLANT

If your handwriting slants to the right, and this is the usual slant found in the majority of people's handwriting, it shows a forward-looking, friendly and sociable disposition. You enjoy human contact and like to have people around you. Because your social instincts are well developed, you are able to forget yourself in thinking of others. Emotionally warm and affectionate, yours is a caring and outgoing personality.

However, if your handwriting slants too far to the right you may be too emotional for your own good; your sociability will be impulsive and spontaneous, but tinged with a lack of caution, because your feelings are near the surface and often run away with you. Eager for new experiences and friendships, you fling yourself into life with enthusiasm.

UPRIGHT SLANT

An upright slant reveals very good self-control, and although you can let your hair down now and then, your head usually rules your heart. Sociable but not sentimental, you don't always show your true feelings and yet they may run deep. You don't go out of your way to meet people but neither do you shrink from mixing with others.

MIXED SLANT

A mixed slant, sometimes left, right or upright, is a sign of changeability and restlessness. You have something of a grasshopper mind and have many and varied friends, but your mood influences your actions and you find it hard at times to keep your friendships on an even keel. Variety and new experiences mean a lot to you. You are impressionable and sensitive to atmosphere and environment, and this can affect your social attitude, as you love being the centre of attention in favourable company.

LEFT SLANT

A pronounced left slant shows an introspective streak; you may have a hang-up about past emotional or environmental experiences that have influenced you. Shy and inclined to be too self-absorbed, you are more interested in your own feelings than other people's.

> Dear Bernie
>
> Just a line t
> You know we are all very
> and we are looking forwar
> you coming home as we ha

This writer has a nicely balanced right slant, showing an outgoing and friendly personality and a need to reach out and communicate. Her rounded script and light pressure shows her to be affectionate and sensitive, with a warm and sympathetic disposition.

> *first of all I tried to*
> *remember how many visitors*
> *came to the garden last*
> *summer and all I could*
> *think of was the fat*
> *woman who dropped her*
> *ice cream cone down my*

Rushing madly to the right, this writing shows a lack of control and discipline. The writer plunges into action and finds it hard to hold back his need for contact. His spontaneity lacks judgment and he is inclined to rush in where angels fear to tread. A highly active man, he is emotional and always in a hurry to get from A to B. His friendships are often fleeting because of this.

> *"The apes yawn & adore their flea*
> *in the sun"*
> *I can't remember any more of it*
> *so that's all!*
> *My name's Carolyn and I live*
> *near Cambridge*

This woman has a slightly left slant, revealing her shyness and reserve; her writing shows her to be a daydreamer living an active inner life. The rounded script and flow of her words show that she is a passive rather than an aggressive personality. The left slant will become a little more upright as she matures and acquires more positive self-confidence. She seeks harmony at any cost in her friendships.

The handwriting analyses doesn't show traits that you would rather not all other people have. I think this is

This narrow inhibited script shows an introspective nature. The writer is putting up a barrier against the outside world and people; his friendships are selective and he is rather aloof. He is defensive and frightened of making contact so assumes an air of singularity, even arrogance, in order to protect his ego.

They want to get engaged personal secrets that they ? themselves. They are also ord themselves and its bad then then feel imprisoned and et I think that parents all over problems and things 1

This rigid writing with its upright rigidity shows a highly inhibited personality. There is a lack of adaptability in the spacing, and the pressure shows a waste of the writer's energy. Her need for emotional and social growth is evident in the small, deflated capital I. Her sociability could be stunted by feelings of inferiority that sap her self-confidence.

Was sample of handwriting analysed at the Franklin Set of Contemporary Studies. For dispatching in out and see

A fluctuating and varying slant shows versatility and an erratic streak. The writer is impatient and intelligent, highly active, and her social attitude is well developed. She enjoys mixing and communicating with lots of people as she enjoys variety and change in her life. She is happy-go-lucky and tolerant towards others.

3
SIZE OF HANDWRITING

The size of your handwriting is highly important in graphology. It reveals your social attitude and how you feel about your friends and family, and how you cope with people.

Because size expresses your personality and personal self-esteem, the graphologist takes this into consideration when analysing for self-confidence and adaptability towards other people. For example, many show business celebrities have extra large handwriting, demonstrating their desire for publicity and their need to be noticed. In contrast, many men of learning bring their handwriting down to a clear uncluttered style.

There are basically three different sizes – large, small and medium handwriting – and each has to be analysed differently.

LARGE HANDWRITING

Very large handwriting belongs to the extroverts and the socially minded people who love the limelight and thrive on attention and admiration. Such writers enjoy showing off and have a strong need for self-expression. They enjoy an active social life with plenty of friends around them. The large writer doesn't seek solitude but enjoys playing to the gallery. There's more than a hint of vanity about them – flattery will get you everywhere with these types.

Large writing is frequently accompanied by a slightly exaggerated ego to match, and it's rare for such writers to be shrinking violets; they usually head committees and organisations. They are not the types to hide their light under a bushel.

SMALL WRITING

The small writer, on the other hand, is more concerned with things than people. Small writing is found in the handwriting of many scientists and intellectuals; researchers, too, often have small writing, as do those who deal with facts and figures.

There's a tendency among small writers to analyse and intellectualise their thoughts and feelings. But when the writing is exceedingly small and cramped the writer may have an inferiority complex; the writer hides his personality behind a façade of caution and reserve. He isn't interested in an active social life, although he can be discriminating in his choice of close friends and acquaintances.

There is a degree of introspection in the small writer's make-up that prevents him from showing off. He shys away from attention, preferring a simple and unpretentious script.

MEDIUM HANDWRITING

Medium handwriting – seen in the handwriting of the majority of the population – shows a good balance between mind and emotion. Such writers don't feel the urge to display an exaggerated ego or conceal their thoughts and feelings, but are socially far more able to communicate and mix, without being either reserved or over-familiar.

This large right-slanted script shows an outgoing and friendly personality, someone who is always looking ahead. The speed of the writing reveals an agile mind and an impatient nature, always in a hurry and hating to be left out of anything. The writer is sociable, hasty in thought and deed, and doesn't suffer fools gladly. The loose rhythm of the script is a sign of a slightly careless type who dislikes too much detail.

in Ipswich. We are liking it here.
We have been to many place around
here, which are very interesting.

Nicely balanced handwriting with a friendly outgoing attitude towards people, this writer is a kindly and sympathetic personality. The rounded script shows a lack of aggression, the light pressure indicating sensitivity and a well-developed social sense.

is a 'Masterpiece', so incredibl
e infact that I was absolute
taunded.

you enclosed a letter

This medium-size handwriting shows a lively, basically non-aggressive personality who enjoys companionship. She is talkative (see the small open a's and o's) and has a friendly approach to people, but the wide spaces between words indicates that she can keep her personal distance when necessary, and in close relationships can be objective as well as affectionate and sympathetic.

and will interested

An exaggerated script such as this huge writing shows a very expansive personality and a lack of reality. Everything is geared to the writer's social life and her interests. She is somewhat selfish and egotistical, with little interest in other people's ideas or opinions. There's far too much emphasis on self, so the writer would have difficulty in understanding other people's problems or needs.

An intelligent and speedy handwriting, this small script reveals a quick-thinking personality. The straightforward capital I tells of an ability to get down to essentials rapidly and without fuss; the thread-like strokes indicate a talent for manipulating and getting on with people. A clever creative writer with a skill for organising and planning. Socially this writer is capable of getting his own way and communicating with ease.

*he named Paris before the knew he was a Trojan.
influenced by the prophetic gift she had received from.
She had to dissuade him from going to find Helen in
Sparta. In spite of his refusal to listen. Oenone told Pa
to come to her if he was wounded, for she had great
skill as a healer.*

An inferiority complex shows itself in this very minute
handwriting with its left slant – always a sign of
reserve and introspection. The lack of dominance
revealed shows that the writer is cautious, doesn't
make friends easily and finds it hard to make himself
one of the crowd. He is far more aloof than he should
be, and could be missing out on opportunities to lighten
his social life because of his shyness.

*. First Marseille has too many memories to
It was where Joe and Lily took the child
before the terrible road accident. Her
boyfriend never got over her death, and
twins wouldn't speak for two months.*

The varying size of letters seen in this sample of
handwriting shows a rather erratic and inconsistent
nature. The writer is intelligent and versatile, but his
friendships are constantly liable to change, and are
subject to mood. There's a lack of rhythm in his writing
and, although he has quite a few loops – always a sign
of emotional lability – he isn't reliable or likely to
maintain steady relationships or friendships. The left
slant adds to his indecisiveness, causing him to be a
little shy about coming forward.

There isn't a lot of handwriting to go on but without asking a sample I can't get any more

Very tall angular writing with spiky strokes tells of a rather sarcastic nature and some in-built aggression. The writer isn't easily pleased, and tries to defend herself by a conscious barrier of reserve, this being emphasised by the pronounced left slant. Her sociability is fraught and far from friendly, this often being the result of disappointment in the sexual area.

4
LETTER FORMATIONS

The way we form our letters gives away many clues to our character. There are four basic letter formations in graphology – angular, thread, arcade and garland. Each one reveals a different kind of personality, and are therefore important in handwriting analysis.

ANGULAR WRITING

There's quite a lot of individuality in the angular script; the lines are sharp and sometimes even pointed, particularly the tops of the small m and n.

Angular writers are shrewd, practical and don't usually make a habit of daydreaming. There's a strong critical streak and when the pressure is quite heavy this shows up in a certain amount of aggression in their nature. They don't suffer fools gladly and are able to concentrate on details with a very observant eye.

Does your handwriting reveal your personality?

— Another of life's imponderables.

There's a rigid and repressive wall of writing showing in this angular script, with its pronounced left slant. The writer is aggressive, with a disciplined movement in his writing, and is inclined to be unsociable. There's a lack of tolerance in the hard strokes, and his emotions are kept well under wraps.

THREAD WRITING

If your writing is inclined to dwindle into threadlike strokes, this is a sign of excellent manipulative ability.

Because you are difficult to pin down, people find you hard to understand; they cannot always come to terms with your elusive personality, which is frequently restless and sometimes erratic. You hate being tied down to one course of action, preferring to feel free to do your own thing when you want to, rather than having to follow a routine.

Your intuition means that you are able to understand other people well, and you have an aptitude for getting your own way without too much trouble. On the positive side you are quick thinking and intelligent; on the negative side you are often secretive, and may juggle with facts to suit your own ends.

Double-thread script is writing that disintegrates into a mere line. In this style you may be lacking in attention to details; you are mentally agile, but your versatility is often wasted through lack of effort. Double-thread writing may also indicate some inner tensions that are disturbing your nervous system so that you are undergoing conflict, either in your emotional or business life. Yours is the most difficult script to analyse, very often because of the illegibility and difficulty in establishing letter forms.

This thread-like writing reveals an evasive writer who likes to use his mental powers but who is inclined to pass over the details and get down to the more important issues quickly. Manipulative and possessing considerable skill in handling people, he isn't always sincere; there are indications in the strokes that he is adaptable but occasionally blurs his character in the process.

ARCADE WRITING

This is a more formal way of writing the letters, and indicates that the writer has a traditional sense of values. They aren't ones for making instant friends, as they like to evaluate before committing themselves. There's often creativity showing in the arcade writer's script, perhaps in the musical area.

Able to keep their own counsel, they rarely let people know their true thoughts and feelings, and yet they are able to communicate and mix well when necessary, even if keeping their personal life to themselves. Their m's and n's will be arched like cathedrals.

This arcade writing, with its arch-like m's and n's, reveals a secretive but creative personality with a good eye for detail. Lacking the easy flow of the thread-writer, there is a more controlled formation, indicating an inner independence and a calm, almost calculating, attitude.

GARLAND WRITING

Because garland writing is an easy script and can be formed quickly, it is often seen in the handwriting of slightly lazy people who are, however, usually friendly, kind and affectionate. They don't have a lot of aggression in their nature, and instead prefer to have harmony in their life rather than friction. It's important too, that they have a fairly active social life, enjoying the company of friends and family.

In particular, they enjoy meeting glamorous people and have a love of interesting surroundings. They make an excellent host or hostess, as this brings out the grand style of their nature. If you are a garland writer your m's and n's will be written like the letter u.

and will be

interested

Garland writing flows along the page easily, often without pressure, showing an amiable nature and a responsive sociability. This writer is outgoing, informal and sympathetic and mild in her approach. She will avoid conflict and is family influenced.

5
THE BASELINE

The way you manage to control the baseline of your handwriting, whether you write on lined or unlined paper, is very important in handwriting.

STRAIGHT

A straight line, without any variation, is a sign of good self-control and discipline. You like to go for a goal without stopping on the way. Your thinking is consistent and decisive, and you are generally reliable and straightforward in your attitude to friends and family.

SLOPING

When your baseline is straight but climbs upwards, this indicates that you are basically an optimistic personality and may be highly ambitious, this impulse to rise being particularly reflected in your social and business attitude. You need to reach out and get to the top. However, an excessively sloping line can indicate excitement and haste; you may be trying too hard to achieve your aims, so that your feelings and hopes run away with you.

When your baseline is sloping down you may be slightly depressed or feeling pessimistic – not too happy with yourself and with life in general at the time of writing. Sensitive and easily hurt, you may have had your feelings bruised, but your depression is only temporary. If your script is also light in pressure, you may be fatigued, this being an additional confirmation that your energy level is low.

STEPS

If the baseline is formed in steps, this indicates that you

have a tendency to be pulled in several directions at once, your emotions being controlled by your moods. This makes you feel up one day, down the next. This inconsistency can cause you to let your heart rule your head one day, your head rule your heart the next.

A more reliable baseline could work wonders for your peace of mind and steady those fluctuating feelings you are often battling with.

CONVEX OR CONCAVE

A convex baseline shows that you are a good self-starter, but you lose your momentum halfway through a project and then have to regain your enthusiasm before finishing the task.

A concave baseline is the opposite, revealing that you are a slow self-starter; you gain more self-confidence as you go along, so that eventually you enjoy the fight and achieve your aims.

WAVY

A wavy baseline indicates versatility and even difficulty in sticking to decisions, showing that you are often open to receive impressions from people and from your surroundings. You are impressionable to external influences, and lack a strong willpower.

Very often there is a touch of creativity in your personality, which needs to be channelled into positive areas.

SUMMING UP

- A straight line across the paper shows good balance between self-discipline and judgment.
- An upward slope reveals ambition, optimism and goal mindedness.
- A downward slope reveals mild depression.
- A step-like baseline shows indecisiveness.

- A convex line reveals a quick self-starter/quick confident finisher.
- A concave line demonstrates versatility and sometimes creativity.

This extremely straight baseline shows a determined and reliable personality. The heavy pressure confirms the writer's strong willpower, and the firm t bars indicate ambition, but also some daydreaming.

The rising lines of the script indicate optimism and a reaching towards a goal. The writing is quick, showing that there is plenty of drive and activity going on in the writer's mind. He enjoys being highly active in his work.

..... us I may be voting in ..it believe it ..ither), I shall cast ..ises to introduce a 72 = hour - to prepare myself for 'A'-levels

This writing dips down at the end – always a sign of mild depression. The writer is inclined to be moody, and the large spaces between lines tell of some apprehension and feelings of emotional isolation. This could be a momentary thing, as the spacing between words is good, showing that the writer has the ability to mix and communicate.

Putting pen to paper is rather

Steps in the baseline indicate that this writer is erratic in her thinking and inclined to let her thoughts and feelings be channelled into several areas at once. She lacks a clear, decisive mind and needs to concentrate more in order to achieve.

How much handwriting is necessary

This convex baseline reveals the quick writer whose mind works rapidly – the rise and then the fall of activity shows how he works.

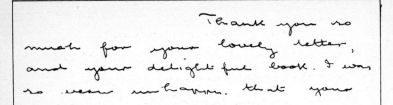

This wavy line of handwriting shows a changeable and versatile writer who is also extremely clever at getting her own way through manipulation.

6
SPEED IN HANDWRITING

The speed of your handwriting can be estimated by the fluency and continuity of your script; disconnected writing is usually slower than writing that is connected and that is therefore made in a continuous motion.

A very fast script shows intelligence and an ability to get down to essentials quickly and without fuss. If you have starting strokes to your words you tend to be slower and more cautious in your approach to life, especially when making decisions; you like to take your time before committing yourself, and may lose out on opportunities through a reluctance to take chances.

If your t bar flies to the right of the stem, this indicates your mental quickness. If you have a habit of linking your words together, this could mean that you are impatient and impulsive, particularly if your writing has a pronounced right slant.

Consistent pressure that doesn't vary is a good sign, showing that your writing speed is constant and that your energy level is neither too high nor too low. Fluctuating rhythm shows inconsistency; although the writer may be versatile and clever, he or she may be erratic and emotionally unstable.

Very large handwriting is rarely fast, as the writer tends to waste time and effort. Small writing, however, is usually very fast and denotes mental agility. It is a fact that the more articulate you are the faster you will write, so fast writing is a clear indication of your verbal talents as well as your mental capacity. In the same way, the more simplified your writing the quicker you will write, and the more elaborate your writing the more time you take over it.

Intelligent writers often depart from the writing style they were taught at school, finding it too slow and cumbersome; they adopt an original and economical form of writing, sometimes eliminating the upper and lower strokes to save time, so that the writing appears to be all middle zone.

Many executives who wield power and authority have small fast writing, but seem to compensate for this with a large inflated and egotistical signature.

Of the population as a whole, 75 per cent have medium-to-slow scripts, only about 23 per cent have exceptionally fast scripts, and about 2 per cent have exceedingly slow copybook handwriting which hasn't developed since their schooldays.

Connected writing and ascending lines are two more indications of fast writing and goal-mindedness.

QUICK WRITING

Positive traits of quick writing:
- Adaptability.
- Spontaneity.
- Enthusiasm.
- Intelligence.
- Mental agility.

Negative traits of quick writing are:
- Neglect of detail.
- Poor concentration.
- Superficiality.
- Rashness.
- Tendency to be influenced by external matters.

SLOW WRITING

Positive traits of slow writing are:
- Steadiness.
- Thrift.
- Consistency.
- Caution.

- Thoroughness.
- Self-control.
- Precision.

Negative traits of slow writing are:

- Passivity.
- Inactivity.
- Lack of energy.
- No quick decisions.
- Self-consciousness.
- Hesitancy.

There's a very quick mind showing in this speedy and connected script. The writer is always in a hurry, impatient, and likely to miss out on minor details in her haste. The right slant and threadlike formation are indications of communicativeness and sociability, while the large spacing between lines indicates good organising ability plus a talent for making quick decisions. The writer is mentally able to grasp situations at a glance and will act with the same amount of speed both emotionally and socially.

ist as an added way explaing my nature myself Does it lie?

This left-slanted and rather large writing is a sign of a more cautious and introspective writer. The carefully formed letters and carefully crossed t bar show a pedantic nature, and a bit of a stick-in-the-mud mentality. It's unlikely that this writer would act hastily or without due thought for the consequences; impulsiveness is alien to her nature.

waiting for my handwriting to be deciphered must in itself tell you something about my

This is the average speed of handwriting, showing a medium-size script, slightly right-slanted, and well-formed capitals. The spacing is nicely balanced and the writing overall shows a capable, intelligent and well-organised individual, able to assess and regulate her speed when necessary.

7
PRESSURE IN HANDWRITING

Pressure in handwriting shows the amount of energy the writer has, and how this is transformed into activity, whether the writer is a high activity person with an emotional nature or is a sensitive rather highly strung individual with a lack of reserve energy to fall back on.

When analysing handwriting pressure it is important to take into consideration the type of pen used; a felt-tip pen will often give the impression of heavy pressure when, in fact, the writing may be quite light. To reveal the true degree of pressure, look at the back of the page; if the indent of the pen shows through, this demonstrates heavy pressure.

HEAVY PRESSURE

Heavy pressure indicates energy and drive – even aggression, occasionally, particularly if the writing is angular rather than round. Such writers are forceful in argument, are doers rather than thinkers, and have a tendency to be over-emotional. Somewhat egotistical, there is a strong need for materialistic success and a certain amount of earthiness in their character. They enjoy eating, drinking and sex, and have strong physical needs. They prefer activity to contemplation, and often work with their hands.

LIGHT PRESSURE

Light pressure reveals a more sensitive personality and a mental alertness, combined with a strong critical streak if the writing is angular.

These writers are easily hurt and may be bruised emotionally. Clever enough to write with the minimum of vitality, they are less volatile and active but can be touchy when frustrated in their aims. Because they dislike unnecessary force or argument, they adapt by means of subtle manipulation rather than hostility.

They are quickly offended by words, and there's often a lack of tolerance in their make-up; when ruffled they can be sarcastic and irritable.

MEDIUM PRESSURE

This is found in the handwriting of the majority of the population, and there is no special significance attached to it. Other signs such as size, slant and formation must be taken into account when analysing such writing.

The medium-pressure writer does show good balance between mind and emotion; there is no desire to overplay or underplay a role. Such writers are usually adaptable, and although they may not be as energetic or highly active as the heavy-pressure writer, they do like to strike an even note in life and don't go for extremes.

ERRATIC PRESSURE

Erratic pressure is a sign of fluctuating moods and emotional disturbances, which combine to upset the writer's control.

There is tremendous drive and a strong ego shown in this heavy pressure and right slant. The writer is impulsive, highly charged emotionally and likes all the good things of life. He doesn't have a great deal of control in his emotional life and is inclined to rush in where angels fear to tread. Energetic and possessing a socially active personality, he shows a need to express his personality in this script.

This fine pressure is a sign of sensitivity, while the left slant indicates reserve and introspection. The writer is aggressive, yet self-absorbed, has a highly critical nature and lacks tolerance as there are few right movements.

This nicely rounded script with medium pressure reveals a sociable and friendly personality, able to mix and communicate well. There is a degree of organising ability in the spacing, and the full underlengths tell of an affectionate and kindly nature.

Fluctuating pressure, as in this specimen of hand-writing, reveals an erratic and unstable personality, given to moods. A hasty temper is demonstrated by the sharp angles, while the blotches show sensuality and uncontrolled feelings that give way to aggression under tension. When pressure is extreme in its fluctuation like this, it denotes misplaced energy and disorganised behaviour; the writer is unable to control his thoughts, actions or feelings, so that they are chaotic.

8
MARGINS

Margins play an important part in graphology. They are helpful in assessing personality traits, showing your attitude towards the world in general and how you react to other people and to social attitudes.

The left margin relates to the past and its influences, while the right margin indicates the future. Margins that are evenly balanced all the way round the page signify a sense of balance, harmony, order and method, and a certain amount of poise and intelligence. Margins can also reveal good organisation or bad planning.

You must always remember, though, that when analysing the space indicated by margins, more than one example of the handwriting should be scrutinised. This is to determine whether the spacing is an habitual writing pattern or a one-off feature.

LEFT MARGIN

If you have a wide left margin, there's a touch of reserve and shyness in your character – you are cautious in the emotional area and in affairs of the heart. You dislike informality.

If your margin is exceptionally wide it can indicate snobbishness and a high opinion of yourself; you are inclined to have an exaggerated ego and tend to be somewhat bossy.

A narrow left margin indicates a sense of thrift. It shows you can practise economy when necessary – financial matters are important to you, as is saving for a rainy day. The material aspects of life colour your thinking; indeed, you can be almost obsessional about money and may even get a reputation for meanness.

RIGHT MARGIN

An irregular right margin is a feature of a writer who has changing opinions and moods, from pessimism to optimism and back; they are inclined to have a grasshopper mind, flitting from one thing to another very quickly. Socially they fluctuate from overactivity to lethargy, but can be exciting to be with. They are rarely boring.

UPPER MARGIN

When the upper margin is wide and has lots of space, it shows a daydreamer who isn't practical. Wide upper margins indicate slightly lazy characters who like to drift a little, occasionally making a great spurt. Such writers sometimes miss out on opportunities through lack of persistence.

In contrast a narrow upper margin is a sign of a compulsive talker who doesn't think of the future. The writer doesn't have a well-developed social sense but is gregarious and friendly – often too familiar. They show a quick mind and lively interests, but often obtrusiveness and poor taste.

BOTTOM MARGIN

The bottom margin is an indicator of emotional and sexual habits, revealing apprehensions or fears about sexual matters. Often this is tied in with past experiences that have influenced the writer.

A narrow bottom margin, for example, is characteristic of a writer who enjoys the good things of life – eating, drinking, sex. It goes with a sensual nature and an active love life.

OTHER CHARACTERISTICS

A well-placed page of handwriting, framed with evenly

sized margins, signifies an ability to plan and organise with skill. It reveals an emotionally and mentally mature personality that is well able to cope with most situations without going into a flap. The writer is usually cool, calm and stable.

In contrast, uneven margins show erratic behaviour patterns on the part of the writer. Unpredictable and inconsistent at times, they reveal an extremely restless nature and a need for constant movement. The writer is easily bored, finding it hard to concentrate and relax, but is affectionate and highly emotional.

No margins at all are characteristic of someone who is stingey, both financially and emotionally. They lack discretion and are likely to waste time, effort and energy. They aren't particularly socially discriminating and, due to poor tact and diplomacy, they often rush in where angels fear to tread.

If you write with wide margins all round you enjoy privacy and are rather withdrawn and snobbish, not wanting to join in and mix or socialise a lot. Such writers aren't keen on team enterprises, but are highly sensitive and critical, with a strong sense of duty.

The writer who actually watches his margins as he writes is a perfectionist; pedantic and highly critical, difficult to get on with and lacking in tolerance, he doesn't suffer fools gladly. A fragile ego makes him take offence easily over real – or imagined – slights.

A page of handwriting filled up completely, without any margins, shows a lack of taste and an unconscious fear that someone may use the writer's space. Elderly people who were taught to practise thrift often write in the margins as a measure of economy.

This wide left margin is a sign of reserve, and yet the right slant shows that the writer can be outgoing and gregarious when she wants to be. The threadlike strokes show great manipulating ability.

No margins at all and a narrow script reveal a stingy nature and poor adaptability. The angular strokes also show mild aggressive tendencies.

> not for any reason
> but I would like
> to know more about
> my personality
> So that I can u so the

These fluctuating lines and uneven margins indicate a restless mind and lack of discipline; the writer is indecisive and her feelings are chaotic.

> How much of my handwriting will it be
> necessary to send you to carry out can analysis
> of my handwriting for various purpose -

A narrowing and erratic right margin is a sign of a versatile but changeable temperament. The writer is intelligent and quick thinking, as the speed of her script shows, but the margin does indicate an inability to stick to routine.

> nipped, over to the
> et up with M + D
> 'Spanish Tragedy'. We
> ll and watched the
> the Olivier where they'd
> d Dolls'. They all came
> running tunes from the
> Spanish Tr-.' "

This wide right margin and disconnected script shows individuality and a dislike of adapting to other people's ideas. There is also apprehension about the future.

9
CAPITAL
LETTERS

The way you form your capital letters gives away how you rate your self-esteem and self-importance; they give indications about your ego. Whether your capital letters are large or small, plain or embellished, they reveal a lot about your true character that you may not know.

STARTING STROKE

A long starting stroke to your capitals means that you are hooked on the past, on its traditions and influences. Breaking away from old traditions and scenes can be difficult, as you cling to what you know rather than venture into the future.

LARGE CAPITALS

Very large capitals indicate that you are a generous but slightly flamboyant personality with a strong need for self-expression in your make-up. You love being the centre of attention and have an expansive nature and a desire for recognition.

You also have a tendency to exaggerate at times in order to impress, and there's more than a hint of vanity in your attitude, which could overtake your good judgment now and then.

Because you dislike being left out of things, family and friends may find you a little overpowering.

SMALL CAPITALS

Small capitals are the opposite and reveal that you may be

suffering from mild feelings of inferiority. You tend to hide your light under a bushel. Not for you the limelight and bags of attention; you prefer a quieter social life, and are inclined to be a trifle shy with strangers.

You may need to assert yourself more in order to achieve your aims and ambitions in life.

MEDIUM CAPITALS

Medium-size capital letters are the average – they are found in the handwriting of the majority of the population. They show a good balance between self-esteem and assurance.

If you use medium-size capitals, then you are neither too bossy nor too submissive, but have a very objective evaluation of your own personality, including your capabilities and potential.

TALL CAPITALS

Very tall narrow capitals show a strong but repressed nature. You are inclined to keep yourself to yourself and don't make friends easily. There is an economical streak that prevents you from wasting time, effort and money, and your emotions are uptight as well.

Lacking in responsiveness, you find it difficult to let go and relax; your inhibitions have a good hold on your feelings, often leading to frustration.

WIDE CAPITALS

Wide fat capital letters are a sign of a wasteful personality, although you are sometimes the happy-go-lucky type, albeit with a streak of laziness. Basically non-aggressive you dislike too much physical exertion and prefer to take the easy way out of situations and relationships.

ANGULAR CAPITALS

Capitals that are angular and rigid reveal poor adaptability and aggression. You have an obstinate and even sarcastic nature, which surfaces when you are angry or frustrated.

It could be that your suffered some opposition and parental control in your youth, and had to put up some resistance against this. Certainly, something you have fought against has caused you to put up barriers, and this influence is hard to break.

ROUNDED CAPITALS

Rounded capitals are indicative of a gentle, affectionate and non-aggressive nature. They show a love of home, of family and of friends. You have no wish to dominate others and have a sense of humour that attracts people to you.

FLOURISHED CAPITALS

If your capital letters are full of whirls and flourishes, then you have a desire to enhance and show off your personality by superfluous mannerisms. You enjoy showing off in front of people and are impressed by money and position. Success and power are all important to you – you like your own way.

This large G indicates an extrovert who wishes to show the world he's an important figure. He needs the limelight, and some tact and diplomacy may be necessary in order to deal with him successfully. He is very conscious of his image.

Tonight

A slight inferiority complex is seen in this small poorly formed capital T. The writer needs to come out of her shell and mix in order to boost her flagging self-confidence.

How

This wide H shows a wasteful and very extravagant nature. The writer is also slightly lazy, and dislikes physical effort.

Many

The angular M reveals aggression and a strong dominant nature. This is confirmed by the triangular underlength of the small y, always a sign of emotional disappointment.

Beverly

The rounded strokes of this B demonstrate a kind friendly nature and a sense of humour. The writer is affectionate and has a warm personality.

The long stroke starting the N shows a busybody and fusspot. This writer is over-cautious, inclined to be hung up about the past, and finds it hard to make a break.

This enrolled and large capital shows a rather vulgar mind and a lack of taste and refinement. The writer is loud, overbearing and somewhat crude.

This plainly written F is simply formed and legible. It reveals an intelligent, well-read and mentally agile personality who dislikes any form of ostentation and has excellent taste.

10
THE CAPITAL I

The way you form your capital I reveals how you value and evaluate your ego. The I is a symbolic sign of self-esteem or self-devaluation and gives away almost as much as your signature. Whether you feel important and confident or pessimistic and isolated, it will show in the way you write this letter of the alphabet.

WHAT TO LOOK FOR

An exaggerated capital I shows that you feel yourself to be important; you may look slightly arrogant, seeking attention and hating to be left out of things. You like to be the boss in any enterprise and have a tendency to show off and be the centre of attraction whenever possible, especially with your friends.

A very small capital I is the opposite; you may have feelings of pessimism or lack the confidence to do the things you really want to do. It could be that you've been repressed a little, either in your family or your emotional relationships, and find it hard to assert your personality.

When your capital I is a straight line down, this shows you to be intelligent, quick thinking and able to get down to essentials quickly and without unnecessary fuss. Emotionally you have good head control and are able to balance what is important and what isn't with excellent judgment. Some people may find you cool, but you just like to keep your emotions under control.

If your capital I swings to the left, or leans to the left, there's more than a hint of a guilt complex preventing you from enjoying life. You may have been under pressure or suffered a disappointment in the past, and this is now affecting your thinking and feelings; letting go of the past will enable you to come to terms with it.

When your I is like a circle, rounded and bold, this shows a sense of humour; you have a sense of the dramatic, although occasionally you retreat into defensiveness when your feelings are becoming too intense. You are a tiny bit apprehensive about making unsatisfactory relationships.

When your I is angular and spiky you may have been thwarted in your ambitions and repressed; you can become sarcastic at times and have a sharp wit. Sincere and strong minded, your likes and dislikes are soon firmly established. You certainly don't suffer fools gladly.

MORE CLUES

An I that is fragmented shows that you love travel and can't stand a restricted environment to live and work in. Because you aren't too firmly rooted in yourself you are often swayed by impulse and spontaneity. You tend to be erratic and undisciplined, both in your emotions and social life, but usually have lots of adventures.

A large loop to your I is a sign of emotion – you are warm, impulsive, sentimental and enjoy an active social life, although you need someone to lean on to feel secure. The more looped your I the more affectionate and loving you are – a true romantic.

An I that is the same size as the rest of your capital letters indicates a good balance between head and heart, but when your capital I is a great deal higher than your other capitals then you could be a really bossy individual who wants to dominate and to make your mark.

When you roll your I in two loops, you are guarding against being hurt; you seek to find harmony, and are sometimes suspicious of other people's motivations. An I that is very complicated shows self-awareness and an analytical mind that likes to unravel problems, thus finding interest in sorting out situations and people.

A printed I shows an interest in literary matters and can indicate creativity along these lines. It can also reveal a more general love of beautiful things and a liking for order and method in your life.

If you enroll your capital I you tend to limit your sociability, but often have a lot of affection and pent-up feelings to give once you let them go and enjoy yourself more.

This large inflated I shows an active and socially aware personality who loves to be in the swing of things, even though the left slant shows that he had to overcome shyness when young.

There's a poor little ego here trying to get out.

Direct, intelligent and well balanced, this straight I indicates self assurance and confidence.

What a lot of guilt this writer is showing in this bowed left I.

Rounded and large, there's humour but also defensiveness revealed.

Angular and rather stark, this writer isn't an easy person to get on with.

Erratic and lacking security within herself, this writer needs to feel more positive about things and make decisions that stick.

An emotional loop this, kind and friendly.

Two loops show impulsiveness, and the right slant is a sign of an affectionate and socially outgoing nature.

A cultured look about this I shows the writer to be intelligent and fond of reading and creative activity.

11
THE DOT OVER THE I

The i dot has a significant part to play in graphology. It can reveal caution and reserve, spontaneity and impulsiveness. Of all the characteristics, it is often the one forgotten by student graphologists, and yet it has its rightful place in handwriting analysis.

THE POSITION

The position of the dot is most important. A dot placed to the left of the stem is a sign of caution on the part of the writer; it shows deliberation before commitment to a course of action, and hesitation when making decisions. In contrast, the i dot that is to the right of the stem indicates that the writer is far more progressive, forward thinking and has a practical turn of mind but, again, shows some reserve.

When the i dot is exactly above the stem but low down, this indicates a good eye for detail and an excellent memory, but very little imagination and creative flair. A very high i dot above the stem shows the dreamer who may have an enquiring mind but who often lacks reality and finds it hard to come down to earth. Such writers also have a rather inquisitive nature and are often imaginative.

When the i dot flies to the right of the stem in a slightly upward slant it shows ambition, enthusiasm, spontaneity and plenty of vision and activity. The writer likes to be busy, and rarely wastes time or effort on non-essentials.

When the i dot is connected to the next letter it shows intelligence, mental agility and adaptability. It is a combination of positive qualities and long-term planning skill.

When the i dot is left out altogether this can be because the writer is such a quick thinker that his thoughts flow before action, or it can reveal carelessness and sloppiness in punctuation.

THE SHAPE

An i dot in the shape of a small elongated line reveals sensitivity and an impressionable nature. The writer is hard to please, is usually critical and inclined to overreact against slights, real or imagined.

An i dot made in the form of a tiny arc shows a well-developed imagination and excellent powers of observation. This particular formation is often found in the handwriting of people who have a creative streak, or who are helping others develop intuition and understanding.

When the i dot is a tiny circle, this shows an offbeat sense of humour. It is frequently found in the handwriting of young girls who have a desire to be different or who want to be thought to be artistic – they use it as a means of self-expression.

An i dot that is extremely large and racing to the right is a sign of restlessness and impatience. Executives and those who have to make hasty decisions frequently show such a dot.

Pointed or sharp arrow-like i dots indicate anger and a sarcastic streak.

A very heavy i dot is often caused by depression and pessimism. The writer is feeling weighed down, and projects a heavy heart in the way he or she forms the i dot.

In contrast, an extremely light i dot signifies a lack of energy and a certain amount of apathy on the part of the writer. But this can sometimes be caused by a fine type of pen, and so has to be carefully checked.

Position

This left-tending i dot shows a cautious and rather fussy nature. The writer lacks impulsiveness and is inclined to be pedantic.

in first

Written above the stem, these i dots are indicative of an excellent ability to work with details and employ powers of observation.

handwriting

Tightly controlled, these i dots indicate a careful, detailed and somewhat reserved nature.

circle

Tiny elongated dashes reveal sensitivity and a well-developed critical sense.

into this

These heavy dots and light writing show mild depression and a pessimistic nature.

tiny little

The little circle shows a sense of humour, and a bid for attention in the non-aggressive handwriting.

thing *thing*

There's more than a hint of originality in this erratic script, while the tiny arc-like i dot shows intuition backed by versatility.

12
THE T BAR

One important facet of your handwriting that can reveal a lot about your personality is the way in which you form a t bar. The positioning of this stroke can give away more than meets the eye, and how you place the bar across the stem of your t shows whether you are self-confident, ambitious, pessimistic, cautious or spontaneous in your thinking.

POSITION

A t bar connected to the following letter is frequently a sign of speed, and usually denotes an intelligent and quick thinking mind. But when the t bar is placed to the left of the stem, this reveals caution and a tendency to hold back, particularly when making decisions; because of this you may not always grasp opportunities.

The t bar that flies away to the right is a sign of an agile mind, impatience and a great emphasis on achieving goals. Often a leadership sign in handwriting, it can show energy and ambition.

The t bar that slopes slightly downwards can indicate anger under tension, but the bar that is slightly upwards on the stem shows a basically optimistic individual. When a t bar is low down on the stem this is a sign to be wary of, as it can indicate depression.

A t bar placed carefully and precisely in the middle of the stem demonstrates a careful, cautious and rather pedantic nature. The writer is not given to impulsive gestures or spontaneous acts; he may lack forcefulness, but has a generally steady and methodical manner.

A t bar at the very top of the stem reveals that the writer may have some ideas or ambitions that aren't too practical, and has a tendency to daydream the time away.

SHAPE

If your t bar is rounded and full, this shows you to be sensitive and impressionable, with a strong need for security and affection.

A long thin t bar which crosses over the entire word can be a sign of protectiveness towards your family and friends, but if it is heavy and the pressure dark it could mean that you are a little intolerant and have a patronising attitude at times.

An angular t bar shows that you may have suffered disappointment in your love life; this tends to make you somewhat touchy under pressure and inclined to give way to irritability now and then.

A t bar that sharpens at the end to the right reveals a quick temper, but a t bar starting with a point and getting thicker shows you are slow to anger.

If you have a tiny hook at the beginning or end you can be tenacious – you like to finish whatever you start. Thoughtlessness is shown in a thick t bar, and sensitivity in a light pressure. If your t bar is knotted it denotes thoroughness and a dislike of interference in your affairs.

---

but

This tall letter t with its low bar shows a writer of high spiritual aspirations and ambitions, but one who suffers from depression, possibly due to lack of realism.

---

character

This rising t bar is a sign of ambition and a basic optimism on the part of the writer; the sharpening point to the right indicates a hasty temper.

The rounded loop to this t indicates emotion, and the right slant shows social needs; the writer is forward looking and gregarious.

A patronising t bar. This sample, with its huge stroke covering the entire word, and the tiny hooks to the right, emphasises the writer's tenacity of purpose.

Cautious and unlikely to act without thought for the consequences, this left-of-the-stem t bar signifies a slightly introverted personality who is frequently caught up in influences from the past.

A triangular t bar denotes a rather aggressive character who doesn't suffer fools gladly and has a quick fuse. This sign is often seen in the handwriting of people who are disappointed with their partner.

13
SIGNATURES

The most important thing you can write is your signature. Of all aspects of your handwriting, it is your signature that reveals most about your personality; the way your signature is formed, the size, pressure and slant, are all indications of your ego, and show how you feel about your place in society as a whole. Whether you are shy and reserved or outgoing and socially minded, egotistical or inclined to be inhibited, the way you write your name tells all.

SIZE AND CLARITY

A rounded legible signature is a sign of honesty and reliability. Usually the writing is right slanted, showing an amiable and friendly personality and an ability to communicate and mix with ease. The more legible your signature, the more open you are liable to be. Illegible signatures can be an attempt to deceive, with the writer desiring to keep his thoughts secretive.

A very small signature is a sign of inhibition, particularly if the letters are squeezed and tightly written. There is a need for protection and safety, with the writer withdrawing into himself and keeping people at a distance.

DECORATION

A signature that is circled around itself is a sign of withdrawal; the writer is afraid of the world and other people, so tries to protect his ego by circling his name as a means of defending himself. This is not a good sign in graphology, and can reveal depression if the pressure is very heavy.

A highly embellished signature, with plenty of whirls and loops, is a sign of a bid for attention. The writer is showing off, and needs admiration and fuss in order to bolster a slight inferiority complex. He is usually loud and aggressive, with a habit of showing off in front of people and making himself known.

Many showbusiness personalities and celebrities in the public eye tend to add a great deal of flourish to their signature, in order to be noticed. In reality, however, they often succeed in a rather vulgar signature, showing their vanity.

The underlined signature demonstrates the man or woman who wants to stamp their personality on the reader. It symbolises a healthy ego and a need for self-esteem. Many executives underline their signature as a means of adding weight to their importance, pointing up their feeling of superiority and authority.

OTHER CHARACTERISTICS

Ascending signatures show a basic optimism, while descending signatures reveal pessimism, especially if they are written with strong pressure and drooping letters.

A dot at the end of your signature means that you wish to cut off quickly; it shows an impulse to come to the end of it without any more ado. A dot is frequently an inhibitive mechanism.

Crossed strokes in a signature are often a sign of anger, or show a sarcastic streak; the writer doesn't suffer fools gladly and likes to be seen as a dominant figure.

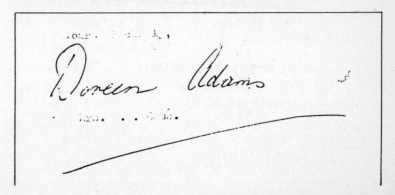

This large signature with its right slant and inflated capitals indicates a healthy ego and need for self-expression. The writer is socially minded and forward looking, but has a slightly exaggerated idea of her own importance.

Yours sincerely

This small varying slanted signature with its poor rhythm shows a very disturbed personality suffering from an inferiority complex, and having great difficulty in maintaining emotional and mental balance.

MIKE ALLEN

Mike Allen shows a quite aggressive signature, with its angular strokes and complicated whirls. The i dot made in the form of a circle is a symbol of egoism, and the underlining stresses his feeling of self-importance.

Mary Short

This left-handed angular signature is very aggressive and dominant. There's a fair amount of energy in the pressure, while the unlooped underlength of the y shows domestic problems and conflict in a sexual area.

Spike Milligan

Spike's signature shows that at some time he may have studied calligraphy. He doesn't give a lot away in this form of writing, although he does show creativity, originality and artistic flair in the original and unusual formation of his letters.

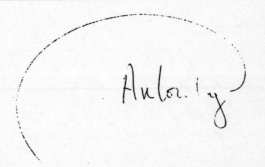

Anthony's half-circle round his name is a self-protecting gesture, a covering stroke, showing that he wants to keep people at bay. The light pressure shows his sensitivity, while the disconnected letters reveal his highly developed intuition.

Wendy Craig has a nicely rounded script without any angular lines, revealing a basically non-aggressive nature and a need for harmony in her life. There is an ability to keep a secret, shown in the tightly closed and knotted small a. A friendly and socially discriminating signature.

When a signature dwindles into a line or lines it shows manipulation and, sometimes, deviousness. The writer is able to persuade and get his own way easily. It is difficult to pin him down; he isn't always sincere, but can be very clever.

14
THE INK AND
THE PEN

The colour of the ink you choose to write with can be revealing – far more, perhaps, than you realise. When you choose one particular colour all the time, it can be a significant guide to your feelings; there are many colours to choose from nowadays, so you can pick one to suit your personality.

Furthermore, there is a wide range of pens available; the type you choose says a lot about your emotional attitude.

- Sensitive people still prefer a fountain pen, as do many executives and those in authority.
- Passionate types go for a thick heavy pen.
- Friendly sorts go for a medium pen.
- Critical and pedantic types opt for a thin-nibbed pen.

BLUE

Blue ink shows that you are basically a non-aggressive personality with a warm, friendly and outgoing nature. You are inclined to be sensitive, and there's a caring side to your nature. You are often employed in areas such as nursing, social work and aiding the less fortunate.

A very bright blue pen shows a more sensitive nature, highly strung and sometimes lacking in physical energy and drive. You are very susceptible to atmosphere, people and places, and may have an interest in spiritual matters. Emotionally you don't care for friendships that are too intense, and instead seek harmony and peace rather than frantic or erratic relationships that may be shortlived. You prefer your friends to keep their distance.

BLACK

Black shows the more dominant executive type of personality. Ambitious and anxious to make a name, you usually like to be in charge of your life, and are often found in a position of authority.

You are emotionally a tiny bit uptight, and don't always give away your true thoughts and feelings. Your head is liable to rule your heart.

RED

Red ink is used by people who have large egos and who enjoy being in the limelight. If you choose red as your favourite colour ink, you have an exaggerated idea of your own image; you love to bathe in admiration, are energetic, emotionally passionate and highly active. Your enthusiasm for new ideas can lead you into odd areas, and you tend to be self-opinionated and lacking in consideration for other people's feelings.

Yours is a passionate and affectionate nature and your love life is often hectic and full of adventure. You have a sexy nature and enjoy the physical aspect of life very much. You don't care for any form of restriction on your emotional feelings, but like to express them fully, sometimes in a dramatic way.

VIOLET

'A time and place for everything' is your motto, and this includes sex. Because you aren't spontaneous or impulsive in this area you can become somewhat boring, and are not a very adventurous lover.

BROWN

Brown ink is frequently used by artistic or creative people who seek attention for their efforts. There is an unusual mixture of insecurity and friendliness in your nature, and you have a tendency to go for unconventional thinking, and even unconventional relationships. But you always keep an eye on your security.

GREEN

Green isn't a favourite colour, although introspective types who wish to retreat into themselves now and again do like to use it. Although you are mentally agile you don't always grasp opportunities as you could do. Emotionally you have a habit of analysing your feelings out of existence.

15
DOODLES

Whether your doodles are round, square or angular, and whether they feature animals, flowers, faces, trains or ships, they all have something to say about you. Doodles are more than just fun drawings – they are psychological diagrams and can reveal quite a lot about your personality and how you think and feel.

If you have any tiny fears or apprehensions, they will show in your doodles; if you are happy, secure and socially minded, all these traits will come through in the way you scribble because doodles are a gateway to our unconscious mind, often releasing tensions and showing our innermost thoughts and feelings.

POSITION

Where your doodle is placed on the page is important as this shows how socially minded or how introspective and shy you are. To the left lies the past and its influences, sometimes keeping you back and preventing you from mixing and making friends because you are too reserved. If your doodle is placed to the right of the page you could be rushing to the future just a little bit too fast and your impatience could actually impede your progress.

A doodle placed bang in the middle of the page shows that you enjoy being in the centre of things and have a healthy social life. But should your doodle be small and cramped it could reveal that you feel people are crowding in on you and you want to hide from them.

ROMANTIC AND AGGRESSIVE DOODLES

The most romantic doodles are self-explanatory: hearts,

flowers, circles and cuddly animals. These tend to be the doodles of a woman rather than a man and show a sentimental, affectionate nature. Aggressive people have a habit of doodling aggressive symbols, while non-aggressive personalities give way to romantic and non-aggressive doodles, expressing their more passive or submissive nature.

ANGULAR

Angular doodles such as arrows, whips, guns and sharp, spiky strokes indicate aggression and even hostility. These are more likely to be the doodles of a man and express the male's love of action and adventure.

TRAVEL

People with a longing to get away and travel to far-off places often doodle ships, planes and trains, a symbolic wish fulfilment in their doodle.

ANIMALS

Dogs, cats and furry animals are a sign of affection and warm-heartedness, and reveal a need for emotional security.

HOUSES AND TREES

Houses and trees can be emotional signposts to the doodler's mind, showing how he or she feels about love, family and friends. Stark, bare houses show apprehension and a lack of love, while heavily decorated houses with a chimney, curtains and a door knocker, show that the doodler feels secure and happy. Large fluffy trees go with a sentimental and generous but slightly lazy nature; bare leafless trees show sarcasm and pessimism.

BOXES

Little boxes can mean that you feel trapped and are seeking a way out. Mazes, puzzles and squares linked together can reveal that you aren't too happy in your relationships or work and need to express your personality more. If you doodle ladders or stars you are ambitious and have your eyes set on high goals and aims.

FACES

Faces are a sign of sociability if they are smiling, happy and drawn full-face. When they are grumpy or distorted they show that you aren't too happy with your social life.

FLOWERS AND PLANTS

Flowers and plants are signs of kindness, sympathy and a non-aggressive, warm hearted nature, the doodler often being wrapped up in home, family and friends rather than the world outside.

There's a clever, constructive mind behind this apparently chaotic doodle. The lines and form are well-drawn and firm, and show an ability to use mental

strategy, and an excellent eye for detail.

The 'filling in' here and there shows some frustration in the doodler's working life but he is extremely quick at solving problems. He doesn't let his emotions get out of hand and likes to maintain orderliness in his life. An exceedingly good organiser and planner, he may be feeling thwarted in his ambitions at the time of scribbling this doodle.

Two basically non-aggressive doodles show a kind, rather romantic personality who often conceals her true thoughts and feelings.

The doodles are clinging to the left of the page, a sign of shyness – she needs to come out of her shell more so that her sympathetic and affectionate nature is directed into more outgoing areas. The tiny circles round the cup and saucer symbolise a ring – always a sign of love without end.

Exciting and glamorous faces are often a wish-fulfil-
ment doodle drawn by young women who have a desire
to be beautiful and alluring.

This doodle is full-face with large appealing eyes and
a wide mouth, indicating sexuality. A complete
romantic, the doodler yearns for a happy ending in her
love life and secretly wants to become the exotic
creature of her daydreaming.

Watching eyes represent a suspicious nature and are
often found in insecure people who don't trust others
easily.

These faces with their half humorous, half sly look
reveal sociability – but only after friendship has been

tested. The doodler is inclined to be reserved and the lack of angular strokes indicates that she is far more emotional than she appears to be on the surface. The closed mouth signifies that she can certainly keep a secret well.

The large, round, fluffy crown of this tree shows a warm, calm, slightly lazy personality. The doodler likes harmony and peace in her life and is not going to enjoy friction or any form of conflict in her relationships. The wide trunk shows generosity and the base line indicates a strong need for security.

BIBLIOGRAPHY

Hearns, Rudolph, S. *Handwriting, An Analysis Through its Symbolism*, Vantage Press, 1966.

Jacoby, H.J. *Analysis of Handwriting*, George Allen & Unwin, 1939

Jung, Carl *Four Archetypes*, Routledge & Kegan Paul, 1959.

Jung, Carl *Man and his Symbols*, Picador, 1964

Jung, Carl *The Integration of the Personality*, Kegan Page, 1940.

Marcuse, Irene *Applied Graphology*, Macoy Publishing, 1960.

Meyer, Oscra *The Language of Handwriting*, Peter Owen, 1960.

Mendel, Alfred, O. *Personality in Handwriting*, Stephen Daye Press, 1974.

Olanova, Nadya *The Psychology of Handwriting*, Wiltshire, 1960.

Olanova, Nadya *Handwriting Tells*, Peter Owen, 1978.

Roman, Klara *Handwriting — A Key to Personality*, Kegan Paul, 1954.

Saudek, Robert *The Psychology of Handwriting*, George Allen, 1925.

Saudek, Robert *Anonymous Letters*, Methuen, 1933.

Saudek, Robert *What Your Handwriting Shows*, T. Warner Laurie, 1932.

Singer, Eric *A Manual of Graphology*, Duckworth, 1969.

Singer, Eric *Personality in Handwriting*, Duckworth, 1974

Sonnermann, Ulrich *Handwriting Analysis*, Grune & Stratton, 1950.

Wolff, Werner *Diagrams of the Unconscious*, Grune & Stratton, 1965.

ADDITIONAL INFORMATION

The Secretary
The Graphology Society
33 Bonningtons
Thriftwood
Hutton
Brentwood CM13 2TL

Patricia Marne is the author of:
Graphology, Teach Yourself Books, Hodder & Stoughton,
1980.

More books from Optima

Dream Dictionary by Tony Crisp.

Based on research into thousands of dreams, Tony Crisp's *Dream Dictionary* is an encyclopaedia of dreams and sleep. Designed to be used as a practical guide to exploring your own dreams, it is also an introduction to the history of dreams and the views of great dream researchers such as Jung, Freud and Cayce.

ISBN 0 356 175162   Price (in UK only) £7.99

All in the Mind? by Brian Roet

Have you a problem that won't go away?

This book offers a key to solving long-term problems: physical, social and emotional. Drawing on his practical experience, Dr Roet shows how the mind plays a major role in causing and maintaining illness, and how many physical and psychological symptoms are messages from the unconscious.

Fixed attitudes and false logic can make us our own worst enemies. Often we worry about things that haven't yet happened, or are upset by other people's problems. By unravelling our thought processes, Dr Roet believes we can start on the road to self-knowledge and recovery.

Fascinating case histories and stories are used to illustrate each point; and the many practical suggestions make this an invaluable handbook for anyone who wishes to break free from a chronic problem and live life to the full.

ISBN 0 356 14571 9   Price (in UK only) £5.99

A Safer Place to Cry by Dr Brian Roet

Under stress? Lacking confidence? Feeling depressed?

During therapy, many people burst into tears as if they have found the only safe place to cry and come to terms with problems that disturb their peace of mind and undermine their physical health.

In his new book, Dr Brian Roet — best-selling author of
All In The Mind? — shows us how we can use therapeutic
techniques to release deep-seated emotions, acknowledge
our strengths and weaknesses, and establish emotional
equilibrium. Drawing upon numerous case histories and
years of professional experience, his reassuring and
practical advice guides us towards new ways to enjoy a
more fulfilling life.

ISBN 0 356 17603 7   Price (in UK only) £5.99

Do-It-Yourself Psychotherapy by Dr Martin
Shepard.

Would you like to understand yourself better? Do you
want to lead a richer, more fulfilled life?

Dr Martin Shepard draws on his long experience as a
professional therapist to present this 'do-it-yourself'
approach that provides a real alternative to formal
psychotherapy. Each chapter focuses on one aspect of
human behaviour and concludes with a series of exercises
designed to give you a clearer understanding of your own
thoughts and responses.

The book is extremely practical, helpful and easy to
follow. It will not only enhance your enjoyment of life, but
save you a fortune in therapist's fees.

ISBN 0 356 15413 0   Price (in UK only) £5.99

All Optima books are available at your bookshop or news-agent, or can be ordered from the following address:

Optima, Cash Sales Department,
PO Box 11, Falmouth, Cornwall TR10 9EN

Please send cheque or postal order (no currency), and allow 60p for postage and packing for the first book, plus 25p for the second book and 15p for each additional book ordered up to a maximum charge of £1.90 in the UK.

Customers in Eire and BFPO please allow 60p for the first book, 25p for the second book plus 15p per copy for the next 7 books, thereafter 9p per book.

Overseas customers please allow £1.25 for postage and packing for the first book and 28p per copy for each additional book.